A Supplication For The Beggars

The English Scholar's Library etc.

No. 4.

A Supplication for the Beggars.

[Spring of 1529.]

The English Scholar's Library of
Old and Modern Works.

[SIMON FISH,

of Gray's Inn, Gentleman.]

A Supplication for the Beggars.

[Spring of 1529.]

Edited by EDWARD ARBER,

HON. FELLOW OF KING'S COLLEGE, LONDON; F.S.A.
ASSISTANT PROFESSOR OF ENGLISH LITERATURE, ETC.,
UNIVERSITY COLLEGE, LONDON.

36, CRAVEN PARK, WILLESDEN, LONDON, N.W.
15 December, 1880.
Limited Library Edition, No. 4.

CONTENTS.

A Supplicacyon for the Beggers   I

A Supplication for the Beggers.

ISSUES IN HIS LIFETIME.
A. *As a separate publication.*

1. [1529. Printed abroad.] 8vo. See title at *p.* 1. Wholly printed in a clear italic type.
2. 1529. [Printed abroad.] 4to. Klagbrieff oder supplication der armen dürfftigen in Engen-landt | an den König daselb, gestellet | widder die reychen geystlichen bettler. [A Letter of Complaint or Supplication of the necessitous poor in England shewn to the King thereof against the rich spiritual beggars] M.D.XXIX. [with a preface by SEBASTIAN FRANCK] Black letter.
3. 1530. [Printed abroad.] 8vo. Supplicatorius Libellus pauperum, et egentium nomine, Henricho VIII. Serenissimo Angliæ regi etc. oblatus, contra quotidianas religiosorum ibidem iniurias et impiam auariciam. Ex Anglico in latinum uersus. M. D XXX.
  In the same type and style as No. 1, and with an engraved framework on the title page that may eventually lead to a knowledge of the foreign printer of both the editions.

B. *With other Works.*
None known.

ISSUES SINCE HIS DEATH.
A. *As a separate publication.*

4. 1546. [London.] Fol. A supplication of the poore Commons. Prov. 21 Chap. ¶ Where-unto is added the Supplication of Beggers. [In the same style and type as No. 3. below, and therefore printed by WILLIAM HYLL.] In the heading the "Supplicacyon of Beggers" is assigned to 1524, which is wrong by five years.
5. 1845. London. 8vo. A Supplicacyon for the Beggers. [100 copies only printed.]
6. 1680. Fol. See WOOD's *Ath. Oxon.* i. 59. Ed. 1813
7. 15. Aug. 1878. Southgate, London, N. 8vo. The present impression.

B. *With other Works.*

8a. 1563. London. Fol. This tract is reprinted, with notes by JOHN FOX in his *Actes and Monumentes etc.*
8b. 1570. London. Fol.
8c. 1576. London. Fol. And so in all later editions of the *Book of Martyrs.*
8d. 1583. London. Fol.
9. 1871. London. 8vo. *Early English Text Society. Extra Series. No.* 13. 1871. "Four Supplications. 1529-1553 A.D." The first of these is "A Supplicacyon for the Beggers written about the year 1529, by SIMON FISH. Now re-edited by FREDERICK J. FURNIVALL."

The Summe of the Scripture.

ISSUES IN HIS LIFETIME.
A. *As a separate publication.*

1. [Winter of 1529-1530. Printed abroad.] 8vo. The only copy at present known is in the British Museum. C. 37. a / 2. The title page is torn off, apparently for the safety of the first possessors.

B. *With other Works.*
None known.

ISSUES SINCE HIS DEATH.
A. *As a separate publication.*

2. 1547. London, W. HERBERT, *Typ. Ant.* i. 616, *Ed.* 1785, quotes an edition by JOHN DAY.
3. 11. Dec. 1548. [London.] 8vo. The summe of the holy Scripture, and ordinarye of the Chrystian teachyng, the true christian fayth, by the whiche we be all iustified. And of the vertu of Baptisme, after the teachynge of the Gospell and of the Apostles, With an information howe all estattes should lyue according to the Gospell very necessary for all Christian people to knowe. ¶ Anno. M.d.xlviii.
  [COLOPHON] : Imprynted at London, at the signe of the Hyll, at the west dore of Paules. By Wyllyam Hill. And there to be sold. Anno 1548. The 11 of Decembre. *Cum Gratia et Priuilegio ad Imprimendum solum.*
  The press mark of the British Museum copy is 4401. b. 2.

B. *With other Works.*
None known.

INTRODUCTION.

IR THOMAS MORE, who at that time was but Chancellor of the Duchy of Lancaster, was made Lord Chancellor in the room of Cardinal WOLSEY on Sunday, the 24th of October 1529.

The following undated work—the second of his controversial ones—was therefore written, printed and published prior to that day, and while as yet he held the lower dignity of the ducal Chancellorship.

❡ The supplycacyon of soulys Made by syr Thomas More knyght councellour to our souerayn lorde the Kynge and chauncellour of hys Duchy of Lancaster.

❡ Agaynst the supplycacyon of beggars.

At fol. xx. of this work occurs the following important passage, which, while crediting the Reformers with a greater science in attack, and a more far-reaching design in their writings than they actually possessed: fixes with precision the year of the first distribution in England of SIMON FISH's *Supplicacyon for the Beggers*, and with that its sequence in our early Protestant printed literature—

For the techyng and prechyng of all whych thyngys / thys beggers proctour or rather the dyuels proctour with other beggers that la[c]k grace and nether beg nor lo[o]ke for none : bere all thys theyr malyce and wrathe to the churche of C[h]ryste. And seynge there ys no way for attaynyng theyr entent but one of the twayn / yat ys to wyt eyther playnly to wryte agaynst the fayth and the sacramentys (wheryn yf they gat them credence and obtaynyd / they then se[e] well the

church must nedys fall therwyth) or els to labour agaynst
the church alone / and get the clergye dystroyd / whereuppon
they parceyue well that the fayth and sacramentes wo[u]ld not
fayle to decay : they parceyuyng thys / haue therfore furste
assayd the furst way all redy / sendyng forth Tyndals trans-
lacyon of the *new testament* in such wyse handled as yt shuld
haue bene the fountayn and well spryng of all theyr hole
heresyes. For he had corrupted and purposely changed in
many placys the text / wyth such wordys as he myght make
yt seme to the vnlerned people / that the scripture affirmed
theyr heresyes it selfe. Then cam sone after out in prynt
the dyaloge of freere Roy and frere Hyerome / *betwene ye
father and ye sonne* [*Preface dated Argentine* (Strasburg), 31
August, 1527] agaynst ye sacrament of ye aulter : and the
blasphemouse boke entytled *the beryeng of the masse* [i.e. *Rede
me and be not wroth* / printed at Strasburg early in 1528].
Then cam forth after Tyndals wykkyd boke of *Mammona*
[*Dated Marburg,* 8 *May* 1528] / and after that his more wykkyd
boke of *obydyence* [*Dated Marburg,* 2 *October* 1528]. In whych
bokys afore specyfyed they go forth playnly agaynst the fayth
and holy sacramentis of Crystys church / and most especyally
agaynst the blyssed sacrament of ye aulter / wyth as vylanous
wordes as the wre[t]ches cou[l]d deuyse. But when they
haue perceuyd by experyence yat good people abhorred theyr
abomynable bokes : then they beyng therby lerned yat the
furst way was not ye best for ye furtherance of theyr
purpose / haue now determined them selfe to assay the
secunde way / that ys to witte yat forberynge to wryte so
openly and dyrectly agaynste all the fayth and the sacramentys as good crysten men coulde not abyde the redyng / they
wolde / wyth lyttell towchyng of theyre other heresyes / make
one boke specially agaynst ye church and loke how that wold
proue.

The previous controversial work produced by Sir THOMAS MORE had
but recently appeared under the title of

¶ A dialoge of syr Thomas More knighte : one of the counsayll of oure souerayne lorde the kyng and chaunceller of hys duchy of Lancaster. Wherin be treatyd diuers matters / as of the veneration and worshyp of ymagys and relyques / prayng to sayntys / and goyng on pylgrymage. Wyth many othere thyngys touchyng the pestelent sect of Luther and Tyndale / by th[e]one begone in Saxony / and by th[e] other laboryd to be brought in to Englond.

[COLOPHON]. Emprynted at London at the sygne of the meremayd at Powlys gate next to chepe syde in the moneth of June the yere of our lord. M.C.C.XXIX. *Cum priuilegio Regali.*

Of this extraordinarily scarce first edition, there is a copy in the Corporation Library, London.

As Sir THOMAS MORE felt it necessary to write this second work, of the *Supplicacyon of Soulys, after* he had composed his *Dialogue* the printing of which was finished in June 1529 ; and as his *Supplicacyon* certainly was written and published prior to his advancement on the 24th October following : it is conclusive that S. FISH's tract had not appeared *before* he was writing the *Dialogue,* and therefore that the date of its distribution must by this internal evidence, be fixed as in the spring or summer of 1529 ; however that date may conflict with early testimony, such as incorrect lists of prohibited books, assigning it to 1524, 1526, etc.

Yet JOHN FOX in his *Actes and Monumentes,* [Third Edition] *fol.* 987, *Ed.*1576, states that was

"Throwen and scattered at the procession in Westminster vpon Candlemas day [? 2nd *February* 1529] before kyng Henry the viij, for him to read and peruse."

We have been unable to verify this procession at Westminster on this particular date, and think that if it had been so, Sir THOMAS MORE would have surely noticed to the *Supplicacyon* while writing the *Dialogue,* the printing of which was in progress during the next four months. He may, however, have thought it necessary to write a special book against S. FISH's tract, with its distinct line of attack as he has accurately stated it.

It will be seen from the Bibliography that this date of the Spring of 1529 quite harmonizes with those of the contemporary German and Latin translations ; which, naturally, would be prompt. It is also not inconsistent with the following allusion at p. 30 to Cardinal WOLSEY's still holding the Lord Chancellorship.

❡ And this is by the reason that the chief instrument of youre lawe ye[a] the chief of your counsell and he whiche hath your swerde in his hond to whome also all the other instrumentes are obedient is alweys a spirituell man.

So much, then, as to the certain approximate date of the publication. FOX is quite wrong in assuming as he does in the following paragraph that this work was the occasion of Bishop TONSTAL's *Prohibition* of the 24th October 1526, *i.e.* more than two years previously.

After that the Clergye of England, and especially the Cardinall, vnderstoode these bookes of the *Beggars supplication* aforesayd, to be strawne abroade in the streetes of London, and also before the kyng. The sayd Cardinall caused not onely his seruauntes diligently to attend to gather them vp, that they should not come into the kynges handes, but also when he vnderstode, that the king had receaued one or two of them, he came vnto the kynges Maiesty saing: "If it shall please your grace, here are diuers seditious persons which haue scattered abroad books conteyning manifest errours and heresies" desiryng his grace to beware of them. Whereupon the kyng putting his hand in his bosome, tooke out one of the bookes and deliuered it vnto the Cardinall. Then the Cardinall, together with the Byshops, consulted &c.

Eccles. Hist. &c., p. 900. *Ed.* 1576.

II.

I: now come to the only authoritative account of our Author, as it is recorded in the same Third Edition of the *Actes and Monumentes &c., p.* 896. *Ed.* 1576.

❡ *The story of M[aster]. Simon Fishe.*

EFORE the tyme of M[aster]. Bilney, and the fall of the Cardinall, I should haue placed the story of Symon Fish with the booke called the *Supplication of Beggars,* declaryng how and by what meanes it came to the kynges hand, and what effect therof followed after, in the reformation of many thynges, especially of the Clergy. But the missyng of a few yeares in this matter, breaketh no great square in our story, though it be now entred here which should haue come in sixe yeares before.

Fox is writing of 1531, and therefore intends us to understand that the present narrative begins in 1525.

The maner and circumstaunce of the matter is this :

After that the light of the Gospel workyng mightely in Germanie, began to spread his beames here also in England, great styrre and alteration followed in the harts of many : so that colored hypocrisie and false doctrine, and painted holynes began to be espyed more and more by the readyng of Gods word. The authoritie of the Bishop of Rome, and the glory of his Cardinals was not so high, but such as had fresh wittes sparcled with Gods grace, began to espy Christ from Antichrist, that is, true sinceritie, from counterfait religion. In the number of whom, was the sayd M[aster]. Symon Fish, a Gentleman of Grayes Inne.

It happened the first yeare that this Gentleman came to London to dwell, which was about the yeare of our *Ex certa* Lord 1525 [*i.e. between* 25 *Mar.* 1525 *and* 24 *Mar.* *relatione,* *vivoque testi-* 1526] that there was a certaine play or interlude *monio pro-* *priæ ipsius* made by one Master Roo of the same Inne Gentle- *coniugis.* man, in which play partly was matter agaynst the Cardinal Wolsey. And where none durst take vpon them to play that part, whiche touched the sayd Cardinall, this foresayd M. Fish tooke upon him to do it, whereupon great displeasure ensued agaynst him, vpon the Cardinals part : In so much as he beyng pursued by the sayd Cardinall, the same night that this Tragedie was playd, was compelled of force to voyde his owne house, and so fled ouer the Sea vnto Tyndall.

We will here interrupt the Martyrologist's account, with EDWARD HALLE's description of this "goodly disguisyng." It occurs at *fol.* 155 of the history of the eighteenth year of the reign of Henry VIII. [22 April 1526 to 21 April 1527] in his *Vnion of the two noble and illustrate families of Lancastre and York &c.* 1548.

This Christmas [1526] was a goodly disguisyng plaied at at Greis inne, whiche was compiled for the moste part, by Master Jhon Roo, seriant at the law. [some] xx. yere past, and long before the Cardinall had any aucthoritie, the effecte of the plaie was, that lord Gouernaunce was ruled by Dissipacion and Negligence, by whose misgouernance and euil order, lady Publike Wele was put from gouernance : which caused *Rumor Populi,* Inward Grudge and Disdain of Wanton Souereignetie, to rise with a greate multitude, to expell Negligence and Dissipacion, and to restore Publike Welth again to her estate, which was so doen.

This plaie was so set furth with riche and costly apparel, with straunge diuises of Maskes and morrishes [*morris dancers*] that it was highly praised of all menne, sauing of the Cardinall, whiche imagined that the plaie had been diuised of hym, and in a great furie sent for the said master Roo, and toke from hym his Coyfe, and sent hym to the Flete, and after he sent for the yong gentlemen, that plaied in the plaie, and them highley rebuked and thretened, and sent one of them called Thomas Moyle of Kent to the Flete. But by the meanes of frendes Master Roo and he were deliuered at last.

This plaie sore displeased the Cardinall, and yet it was neuer meante to hym, as you haue harde, wherfore many wisemen grudged to see hym take it so hartely, and euer the Cardinall saied that the kyng was highly displeased with it, and spake nothyng of hymself.

There is no question as to the date of this "disguisyng." Archbishop WARHAM on the 6th February 1527, wrote to his chaplain, HENRY GOLDE, from Knolle that he "Has received his letters, dated London, 6 Feb., stating that Mr. Roo is committed to the Tower for making a certain play. Is sorry such a matter should be taken in earnest." *Letters &c. HENRY VIII.* Ed. by J. S. BREWER, *p.* 1277. *Ed.* 1872.

It would seem however that FISH either did not go or did not stay lonᵍ abroad at this time. STRYPE (*Eccles. Mem.* I. *Part* II, *pp.* 63-5. *Ed.* 1822) has printed, from the Registers of the Bishops of LONDON, the Confession in 1528 of ROBERT NECTON (a person of position, whose brother became Sheriff of Norwich in 1530), by which it appears that during the previous eighteen months, that is from about the beginning of 1527, our Author was "dwellyng by the Wight Friars in London ;" and was actively engaged in the importation and circulation of TYNDALE's *New Testaments*, a perfectly hazardous work at that time.

Possibly this Confession was the occasion of a first or a renewed flight by FISH to the Continent, and therefore the ultimate cause of the present little work in the following year.

We now resume FOX's account, which was evidently derived from FISH's wife, when she was in old age.

Vpon occasion wherof the next yeare folowyng this booke was made (being about the yeare 1527) and so not long after in the yeare (as I suppose) 1528 [*which by the old reckoning ended on the 24 Mar. 1529*]. was sent ouer to the Lady Anne Bulleyne, who then lay at a place not farre from the Court. Which booke her brother seyng in her hand, tooke it and read it, and gaue it [to] her agayne, willyng her earnestly to giue it to the kyng, which thyng she so dyd.

This was (as I gather) about the yeare of our Lord 1528 [-1529].

The kyng after he had receaued the booke, demaunded of her "who made it." Whereunto she aunswered and sayd, "a certaine subiect of his, one Fish, who was fled out of the Realme for feare of the Cardinall."

After the kyng had kept the booke in his bosome iij. or iiij. dayes, as is credibly reported, such knowledge was giuen by the kynges seruauntes to the wife of ye sayd Symon Fishe, yat she might boldly send for her husband, without all perill or daunger. Whereupon she thereby beyng incouraged, came first and made sute to the kyng for the safe returne of her husband. Who vnderstandyng whose wife she was, shewed a maruelous gentle and chearefull countenaunce towardes her, askyng "where her husband was." She aunswered, "if it like your grace, not farre of[f]." Then sayth he, "fetch him, and he shal come and go safe without perill,

and no man shal do him harme," saying moreouer, " that hee
had [had] much wrong that hee was from her so long : " who
had bene absent now the space of two yeares and a halfe,

Which from Christmas 1526 would bring us to June 1529, which cor-
roborates the internal evidence above quoted. FOX evidently now
confuses together two different interviews with the King. The first at
the Court in June 1529 ; the other on horseback with the King, followed
afterwards by his Message to Sir T. MORE in the winter of 1529–30,
within six months after which S. FISH dies. His wife never would have
been admitted to the Court, if she had had a daughter ill of the plague at
home.

In the whiche meane tyme, the Cardinall was deposed,
as is aforeshewed, and M[aster]. More set in his place of the
Chauncellourshyp.

Thus Fishes wife beyng emboldened by the kynges wordes,
went immediatly to her husband beyng lately come ouer,
and lying priuely within a myle of the Court, and brought
him to the kyng : which appeareth to be about the yeare of
our Lord. 1530.

When the kyng saw hym, and vnderstood he was the
authour of the booke, he came and embraced him with louing
countenance ; who after long talke : for the space of iij. or
iiij. houres, as they were ridyng together on huntyng, at
length dimitted him, and bad him "take home his wife, for
she had taken great paynes for him." Who answered the
kyng agayne and sayd, he " durst not so do, for fear of Syr
Thomas More then Chauncellor, and Stoksley then Bishop
of London. This seemeth to be about the yeare of our
Lord. 1530.

This bringing in of STOKESLEY as Bishop is only making confusion
worse confounded. STOKESLEY was consecrated to the see of London
on the 27th Nov. 1530. By that time, S. FISH had died of the plague
which occurred in London and its suburbs in the summer of 1530 ; and
which was so severe, that on 22nd June of that year, the King prorogued the
Parliament to the following 1st October. *Letters &c. HENRY VIII.*
Ed. by J. S. BREWER, M.A., IV, Part 3, No. 6469. *Ed.* 1876.

The Martyrologist, throughout, seems to be right as to his facts, but
wrong as to his dates.

The kyng takyng his signet of[f] his finger, willed hym to haue hym reommended to the Lord Chauncellour, chargyng him not to bee so hardy to worke him any harme.

Master Fishe receiuyng the kynges signet, went and declared hys message to the Lord Chauncellour, who tooke it as suffi-cient for his owne discharge, but asked him " if he had any thynge for the discharge of his wife : " for she a litle before had by chaunce displeased the Friers, for not sufferyng them to say their Gospels in Latine in her house, as they did in others, vnlesse they would say it in English. Whereupon the Lord Chauncellour, though he had discharged the man, yet leauyng not his grudge towardes the wife, the next morning sent his man for her to appeare before hym : who, had it not bene for her young daughter, which then lay sicke of the plague, had bene lyke to come to much trouble.

Of the which plague her husband, the said Master Fish deceasing with in half a yeare, she afterward maryed to one Master James Baynham, Syr Alexander Baynhams sonne, a worshypful Knight of Glo[uce]stershyre. The which foresayd Master James Baynham, not long after, [1 May 1532] was burned, as incontinently after in the processe of this story, shall appeare.

And thus much concernyng Symon Fishe the author of the *booke of beggars*, who also translated a booke called *the Summe of the Scripture* out of the Dutch [*i.e. German*].

Now commeth an other note of one Edmund Moddys the kynges footeman, touchyng the same matter.

This M[aster]. Moddys beyng with the kyng in talke of religion, and of the new bookes that were come from beyond the seas, sayde " if it might please hys grace, he should see such a booke, as was maruell to heare of." The kyng de-maunded " what they were." He sayd, " two of your Merchauntes, George Elyot, and George Robinson." The kyng [ap]poynted a tyme to speake with them. When they came before his presence in a priuye [*private*] closet, he demaunded " what they had to saye, or to shew him"   One of them said "yat there was a boke come to their hands, which they were there to shew his grace."   When he saw it, hee demaunded " if any of them could read it."   "Yea" sayd George Elyot, "if it please your grace to heare it,"   " I thought so " sayd the kyng, " for if neede were thou canst say it without booke."

The whole booke beyng read out, the kyng made a long pause, and then sayd, " if a man should pull downe an old stone wall and begyn at the lower part, the vpper part thereof might chaunce to fall vpon his head : " and then he tooke the booke and put it into his deske, and commaunded them vpon their allegiance, that they should not tell to any man, that he had sene the booke.

III.

O this account we may add two notices.   Sir T. MORE replying in his *Apology* to the " Pacifier" [CHRISTOPHER SAINT GERMAIN] in the spring of 1533, gives at *fol.* 124, the following account of our Author's death—

And these men in the iudgement of thys pytuouse pacyfyer be not dyscrete / but yet they haue he sayth a good zele though.   And thys good zele hadde, ye wote well, Simon Fysshe when he made the supplycacyon of beggers. But god gaue hym such grace afterwarde, that he was sory for that good zele, and repented hym selfe and came into the chyrche agayne, and forsoke and forsware all the whole hyll of those heresyes, out of whiche the fountayne of that same good zele sprange.   [Also at *p.* 881, *Workes. Ed.* 1557.]

This is contrary to the tenour of everything else that we know of the man : but Sir T. MORE, possessing such excellent means of obtaining information, may nevertheless be true.

Lastly. ANTHONY à WOOD in his *Ath. Oxon.* i. 59, *Ed.* 1813, while giving us the wrong year of his death, tells us of his place of burial.

At length being overtaken by the pestilence, died of it in fifteen hundred thirty and one, and was buried in the church of St. Dunstan (in the West).

TYNDALE had often preached in this church.

I V.

HAT a picture of the cruel, unclean and hypocritical monkery that was eating at the heart's core of English society is given to us in this terse and brave little book? Abate from its calculations whatever in fairness Sir T. MORE would have wished us to deduct; we cannot but shudder as we try to realize the then social condition of our country; and all the more, when we remember that the fountain of all this unmercifulness, impurity and ignorance was found in the very persons who professed to be, and who should have been the Divine Teachers of our nation. It argues, too, much for the virility of the English race, that it could have sustained, in gradually increasing intensity, such a widespread mass of festering and corroding blotches of vice, and could by and bye throw it off altogether; so that in subsequent ages no other nation has surpassed us in manhood.

It is marvellous to us how the ecclesiastical fungus could have ever so blotted out of sight both the royal prerogative and the people's liberties. Was not HENRY VIII the man for this hour? A bold lusty and masterful one, imperious and impatient of check, full of the animal enjoyment of life; yet a remarkable Theologian, a crafty Statesman, a true Englishman. Often referred to in the literature of this time as "our Lord and Master." Had England ever had such a Master! ever such a Lord of life and limb since? A character to the personal humouring and gratification of whom, such an one as WOLSEY devoted his whole soul and directed all the powers of the State.

How necessary was so strong a ruler for our national disruption with Rome! It is not easy for us to realize what an amazingly difficult thing that wrench was. MODDYS' story witnesses to us of the King's great perplexity. By what difficult disillusions, what slow and painful thoughtfulness did HENRY's mind travel from the *Assertio* of 1522 and the consequent *Defensor fidei*, to the destruction of the monasteries in 1536. Truly, if in this " passion " he vacillated or made mistakes; we may consider the inherent difficulty of disbelief in what—despite its increasing corruptions—had been the unbroken faith of this country for a thousand years.

We call the disillusionists, the Reformers; but FISH describes them as

men of greate litterature and iudgement that for the love they haue vnto the trouth and vnto the comen welth haue not feared to put theim silf ynto the greatest infamie that may be, in abiection of all the world, ye[a] in perill of deth to declare theyre oppinion. . . . *p.* 10.

Undoubtedly HENRY personally was the secular Apostle of the first phase of our Reformation. The section of doctrinal Protestants was politically insignificant : and it may be fairly doubted whether the King could have carried the nation with him, but that in the experience of every intelligent Englishman, the cup of the iniquity of the priesthood was full to overflowing. He was aided by the strong general reaction of our simple humanity against the horrid sensuality, the scientific villany offered to it by the supposed special agents of Almighty GOD in the name of, and cloaked under the authority believed to have been given to them from the ever blessed Trinity.

Morality is the lowest expression of religion, the forerunner of faith. No religion can be of GOD which does not instinctively preassume in its votaries the constant striving after the highest and purest moral excellence. It is an intolerable matter, beyond all possible sufferance, when religion is made to pander to sensuality and extortion. How bitter a thing this was to this barrister of Gray's Inn, may be seen in the strange terms of terror and ravin with which he characterizes these "strong, puissant, counterfeit holy, and idle beggars." To the untravelled Englishman of Henry VIII's reign, "cormorants" must have meant some like devouring griffins, and "locusts" as a ruthless irremediable and fearful plague without end. By such mental conceptions of utter desolation, impoverishment and misery does our Author express the bitterness of the then proved experience by Englishmen, of the combined hierarchy and monkery of Rome.

All which is for our consideration in estimating the necessity and policy of the subsequent suppression of the monasteries.

These representations are also some mitigation of what is sometimes thought to be the Protestant frenzy of our great Martyrologist, whose words of burning reprobation of the Papal system of his time seem often to us to be extravagant ; because, by the good providence of GOD, we are hardly capable of realizing the widespread and scientific villany of the delusions and enormities against which he protested.

The English Scholar's Library
of Old and Modern Works.

OLD SERIES.

LIMITED LIBRARY EDITION.

In Sets only; of which but 257 are printed.

No. 4.

[SIMON FISH,
of Gray's Inn, Gentleman.]

A Supplication for the Beggars, &c.

[Spring of 1529.]

LIMITED LIBRARY EDITION.

29 ... ... ALEXANDER B. STEWART, Esq., *Buchanan street, Glasgow.*
30 ... . EDWARD ADAMSON, Esq., M.D., *Rye, Sussex.*
31 ... ... THOMAS CHORLTON, Esq., *Brazennose street, Manchester.*
32 ... ... THE MITCHELL LIBRARY, GLASGOW, *Ingram street East, Glasgow.*
33 ... ... F. DE M. LEATHES, Esq., *Tavistock place, London, W.C.*
34 ... ... ARTHUR CHAMBERLAIN, Esq., *Moor Green Hall, Moseley, Birmingham.*
35 ... ... RICHARD CHAMBERLAIN, Esq., *Edgbaston, Birmingham.*
36 ... ... THE LIBRARY OF UNIVERSITY COLLEGE, LONDON, *Gower street, London, W.C.*
37 ... ... WALTER C. RENSHAW, Esq., *Lincoln's Inn, London, W.C.*
38 ... ... C. H. EVERARD, Esq., *Eton College, Windsor.*
39 ... ... CORNELIUS PAINE, Esq., *Kemp Town, Brighton.*
40 ... ... BIRMINGHAM FREE LIBRARIES — REFERENCE DEPARTMENT, *Eden place, Birmingham.*
41 ... Rev. STOPFORD A. BROOKE, *Manchester square, London, W.*
42 ... HORACE HOWARD FURNESS, Esq., *West Washington square, Philadelphia, Pennsylvania, U.S.A.*
43 ... ...The Rt. Hon. the EARL OF DERBY, *Knowsley, Prescot.*
44 ... ... HENRY MERE ORMEROD, Esq., *Clarence street, Manchester.*
45 ... ...
46 ... ...
47 ... ...
48 ... ...
49 ... ...
50 ... ...
51 ... ...
52 ... ...
53 ... ...
54 ... ...
55 ... ...
56 ... ...
57 ... ...
58 ... ...
59 ... ...
60 ... ...
61 ... ...
62 ... ...

SUBSCRIBERS TO THE

102 ... .
103 ... .
104 ... .
105 ... .
106 ... .
107 ... .
108 ... .
109 ... .
110 ... .
111 .. ..
112 ... .
113 ... .
114 ... .
115 ... .
116 ... .
117 ... .
118 ... .
119 ... .
120 ... .
121 ... .
122 ... .
123 ... .
124 ... .
125 ... .
126 ... .
127 ... .
128 ... ., ...
129 ... .
130 ... .
131 ... .
132 ... .
133 ... .
134 ... .
135 ... .
136 ... .
137 ... .
138 ... .
139 ... .
140 ... .

180 ... ...h ... ...
181 ... ...
182 ... ...
183 ... ...
184 ... ...
185 ... ...
186 ... ...
187 ... ...
183 ... ...
189 ... ...
190 ... ...
191 ... ...
192 ... .: ... ...
193 ... ...
194 ... ...
195 ... ...
196 ... ...
197 ... ...
198 ... ...
199 ... ...
200 ... ...
201 ... ...
202 ... ...
203 ... ...
204 ... ...
205 .. ..
206 ... ...
207 ... ...
208 ... ...
209 ... ...
210 ... ...
211 ... ...
212 ... ...
213 ... ...
214 ... ...
215 ... ...
216 ... ...
217 ... .
218 ... ...

219 ... ...
220 ... ...
221 ... ...
222 ... ...
223 ... ...
224 ... ...
225 ... ...
226 ... ...
227 ... .
228 ... ...
229 ... ...
230 ... ...
231 ... ...
232 ... ...
233 ... ...
234 ... ...
235 ... ...
236 ... ...
237 ... ...
238 ... ...
239 ... ...
240 ... ...
241 ... ...: ... ...
242 ... ...
243 ... ...
244 ... ...
245 ... ...
246 ... ...
247 ... ...
248 ... ...
249 ... ...
250 ... ...
251 ... ... THE BRITISH MUSEUM, *London.*
252 ... ... THE ADVOCATES' LIBRARY, *Edinburgh.*
253 ... ... THE NATIONAL LIBRARY OF IRELAND, *Dublin.*
254 ... ... THE BODLEIAN LIBRARY, *Oxford.*
255 ... ... THE UNIVERSITY LIBRARY, *Cambridge.*
256 ... . EDWARD ARBER, Esq., *the EDITOR.*
257 ... ... Messrs. UNWIN Bros., *the PRINTERS.*

⁋ A Supplicacyon for the Beggers.

TO THE KING OVRE

souereygne lorde.

Ost lamentably compleyneth theyre wofull mysery vnto youre highnes youre poore daily bedemen the wretched hidous monstres (on whome scarcely for horror any yie dare loke) the foule vnhappy sorte of lepres, and other sore people, nedy, impotent, blinde, lame, and sike, that live onely by almesse, howe that theyre nombre is daily so sore encreased that all the almesse of all the weldisposed people of this youre realme is not halfe ynough for to susteine theim, but that for verey constreint they die for hunger. And this most pestilent mischief is comen vppon youre saide poore beedmen by the reason that there is yn the tymes of youre noble predecessours passed craftily crept ynto this your realme an other sort (not of impotent but) of strong puissaunt and counterfeit holy, and ydell beggers and vacabundes whiche syns the tyme of they.e first entre by all the craft and wilinesse of Satan are nowe encreased vnder your sight not onely into a great nombre, but also ynto a kingdome. These are (not the herdes, but the rauinous wolues going in herdes clothing deuouring the flocke) the Bisshoppes, Abbottes, Priours, Deacons, Archedeacons, Suffraganes, Prestes, Monkes Chanons, Freres, Pardoners and Somners. And who is abill to nombre this idell rauinous sort whiche (setting all laboure a side) haue begged so importunatly that they haue gotten ynto theyre hondes more then the therd part of all youre Realme. The goodliest lordshippes, maners, londes, and territories, are theyrs. Besides this they haue the tenth part of all the corne, medowe, pasture, grasse, wolle, coltes, calues, lambes,

pigges, gese, and chikens. Ouer and bisides the tenth part
of euery seruauntes wages the tenth part of the wolle, milke,
hony, waxe, chese, and butter. Ye[a] and they loke so narowly
vppon theyre proufittes that the poore wyues must be countable
to theym of euery tenth eg or elles she gettith not her ryghtes
at ester shalbe taken as an heretike. hereto haue they theire
foure offering daies. whate money pull they yn by probates
of testamentes, priuy tithes, and by mennes offeringes to
theyre pilgremages, and at theyre first masses? Euery man and
childe that is buried must pay sumwhat for masses and diriges
to be song for him or elles they will accuse the de[a]des frendes
and executours of heresie. whate money get they by mortu-
aries, by hearing of confessions (and yet they wil kepe therof no
counceyle) by halowing of churches altares superaltares
chapelles and belles, by cursing of men and absoluing theim
agein for money? what a multitude of money gather the
pardoners in a yere? Howe moche money get the Somners
by extorcion yn a yere, by assityng the people to the commis-
saries court and afterward releasing th[e]apparaunce for
money? Finally, the infinite nombre of begging freres whate
get they yn a yere? Here if it please your grace to marke
ye shall se a thing farre out of ioynt. There are withyn
youre realme of Englond. lij. thousand parisshe churches.
And this stonding that there be but tenne houshouldes yn
euery parisshe yet are there fiue hundreth thousand and
twenty thousand houshouldes. And of euery of these houshouldes hath euery of the fiue ordres of freres a peny a quarter
for euery ordre, that is for all the fiue ordres fiue pens a
quarter for every house. That is for all the fiue ordres. xx.d,
a yere of euery house. Summa fiue hundreth thousand and
twenty thousand quarters of angels.
    That is. cclx. thousand half angels. Summa. cxxx. thousand
angels. Summa totalis. xliij. thousand poundes and. cccxxxiij.
li. vi.s. viij.d. sterling. wherof not foure hundreth yeres
passed they had not one peny. Oh greuous and peynfull exactions thus yerely to be paied. from the whiche the people
of your nobill predecessours the kinges of the auncient
Britons euer stode fre And this wil they haue or els they
wil procure him that will not giue it theim to be taken as an
heretike. whate tiraunt euer oppressed the people like this
cruell and vengeable generacion? whate subiectes shall be

abill to helpe theire prince that be after this facion yerely
polled? whate good christen people can be abill to socoure vs
pore lepres blinde sore, and lame, that be thus yerely
oppressed? Is it any merueille that youre people so compleine
of pouertie? Is it any merueile that the taxes fiftenes and
subsidies that your grace most tenderly of great compassion
hath taken emong your people to defend theim from the
thretened ruine of theire comon welth haue bin so
sloughtfully, ye[a] painfully leuied? Seing that almost the
vtmost peny that mought haue bin leuied hath ben gathered
bifore yerely by this rauinous cruell and insatiabill generacion
The danes nether the saxons yn the time of the auncient
Britons shulde neuer haue ben abill to haue brought theire
armies from so farre hither ynto your lond to haue conquered it
if they had had at that time suche a sort of idell glotons to finde
at home. The nobill king Arthur had neuer ben abill to haue
caried his armie to the fote of the mountaines to resist the
coming downe of lucius the Emperoure if suche yerely exac-
tion had ben taken of his people. The grekes had neuer ben
abill to haue so long continued at the siege of Troie if they had
had at home suche an idell sort of cormorauntes to finde.
The auncient Romains had neuer ben abil to haue put all the
hole worlde vnder theyre obeisaunce if theyre people had byn
thus yerely oppressed. The Turke nowe yn youre tyme
shulde neuer be abill to get so moche grounde of cristendome
if he had yn his empire suche a sort of locustes to deuoure his
substance. Ley then these sommes to the forseid therd part of
the possessions of the realme that ye may se whether it drawe
nighe vnto the half of the hole substaunce of the realme or
not, So shall ye finde that it draweth ferre aboue. Nowe
let vs then compare the nombre of this vnkind idell sort vnto
the nombre of the laye people and we shall se whether it be
indifferently shifted or not that they shuld haue half.

Compare theim to the nombre of men, so are they not the.
C. person. Compare theim to men wimen and children, then
are they not the. CCCC. parson yn nombre. One part therfore yn foure hundreth partes deuided were to moche for
theim except they did laboure. whate an vnequal burthen is it
that they haue half with the multitude and are not the. CCCC.
parson of theire nombre? whate tongue is abill to tell that
euer there was eny comon welth so sore oppressed sins the
worlde first began?

⁋ And whate do al these gredy sort of sturdy idell holy theues witn these yerely exactions that they take of the people ? Truely nothing but exempt theim silues from th[e]obedience of your grace. Nothing but translate all rule power lordishippe auctorite obedience and dignite from your grace vnto theim. Nothing but that all your subiectes shulde fall ynto disobedience and rebellion ageinst your grace and be vnder theim. As they did vnto your nobill predecessour king Iohn : whiche forbicause that he wolde haue punisshed certeyn traytours that had conspired with the frenche king to haue deposed him from his crowne and dignite (emong the whiche a clerke called Stephen whome afterward ageinst the kinges will the Pope made Bisshoppe of Caunterbury was one) enterdited his Lond. For the whiche mater your most nobill realme wrongfully (alas for shame) hath stond tributary (not vnto any kind temporall prince, but vnto a cruell deuelisshe bloudsupper dronken in the bloude of the sayntes and marters of christ) euersins. Here were an holy sort of prelates that thus cruelly coude punisshe suche a rightuous kinge, all his realme, and succession for doing right.

⁋ Here were a charitable sort of holy men that coude thus enterdite an hole realme, and plucke awey th[e]obedience of the people from theyre naturall liege lorde and kinge, for none other cause but for his rightuousnesse. Here were a blissed sort not of meke herdes but of bloudsuppers that coude set the frenche king vppon suche a rightuous prince to cause hym to lose his crowne and dignite to make effusion of the bloude of his people, oneles this good and blissed king of greate compassion, more fearing and lamenting the sheding of the bloude of his people then the losse of his crowne and dignite agaynst all right and conscience had submitted him silf vnto theym. O case most horrible that euer so nobill a king Realme, and succession shulde thus be made to stoupe to suche a sort of bloudsuppers. where was his swerde, power, crowne, and dignitie become wherby he mought haue done iustice yn this maner ? where was their obedience become that shuld haue byn subiect vnder his highe power yn this mater ? Ye[a] where was the obedience of all his subiectes become that for mainteinaunce of the comon welth shulde haue holpen him manfully to haue resisted

these bloudsuppers to the shedinge of theyre bloude? was
not all to gither by theyre polycy translated from this good
king vnto theim.   Ye[a] and what do they more?   Truely
nothing but applie theym silues by all the sleyghtes they
may haue to do with euery mannes wife, euery mannes
doughter and euery mannes mayde that cukkoldrie and
baudrie shulde reigne ouer all emong your subiectes, that no
man shulde knowe his owne childe that theyre bastardes
might enherite the possessions of euery man to put the right
begotten children clere beside theire inheritaunce yn subuersion
of all estates and godly ordre.   These be they that by theire
absteyning from mariage do let the generation of the people
wher by all the realme at length if it shulde be continued
shall be made desert and inhabitable.

¶ These be they that haue made an hundreth thousand
ydell hores yn your realme whiche wolde haue gotten theyre
lyuing honestly, yn the swete of theyre faces had not theyre
superfluous rychesse illected theym to vnclene lust and ydelnesse.   These be they that corrupt the hole generation of
mankind yn your realme, that catche the pokkes of one
woman. and bere theym to an other, that be brent wyth one
woman, and bere it to an other, that catche the lepry of one
woman, and bere it to an other, ye[a]some one of theym shall
bo[a]st emong his felawes that he hath medled with an hundreth
wymen.   These be they that when they haue ones drawen
mennes wiues to such incontinency spende awey theire
husbondes goodes make the wimen to runne awey from theire
husbondes, ye[a], rynne awey them silues both with wif and
goods, bring both man wife and children to ydelnesse theft
and beggeri.

¶] Ye[a] who is abill to nombre the greate and brode
botomles occean see full of euilles that this mischtuous and
sinful generacion may laufully bring vppon vs vnponisshed.
where is youre swerde, power, crowne, and dignitie, become
that shuld punisshe (by punisshement of deth euen as other
men are punisshed) the felonies, rapes, murdres, and
treasons committed by this sinfull generacion? where is
theire obedience become that shulde be vnder your hyghe
power yn this mater? ys not all to gither translated and
exempt from your grace vnto theim? yes truely. whate an
infinite nombre of people might haue ben encreased to haue

peopled the realme if these sort of folke had ben maried like
other men. what breche of matrimonie is there brought yn
by theim? suche truely as was neuer sins the worlde began
emong the hole multitude of the hethen.

❡ who is she that wil set her hondes to worke to get.
iij.d. a day and may haue at lest. xx.d. a day to slepe an
houre with a frere, a monke, or a prest? what is he that
wolde laboure for a grote a day and may haue at lest. xij.d. a
day to be baude to a prest, a monke, or a frere? whate a sort
are there of theime that mari prestes souereigne ladies but to
cloke the prestes yncontinency and that they may haue a
liuing of the prest theime silues for theire laboure? Howe
many thousandes doth suche lubricite bring to beggery theft
and idelnesse whiche shuld haue kept theire good name and
haue set theim silues to worke had not ben this excesse
treasure of the spiritualtie? ? whate honest man dare take
any man or woman yn his seruice that hath ben at suche a
scole with a spiritual man? Oh the greuous shipwrak of
the comon welth, whiche yn auncient time bifore the coming
yn of these rauinous wolues was so prosperous: that then
there were but fewe theues: ye[a] theft was at that tyme so
rare that Cesar was not compellid to make penalte of deth
vppon felony as your grace may well perceyue yn his institutes.
There was also at that tyme but fewe pore people and yet
they did not begge but there was giuen theim ynough
vnaxed, for there was at that time none of these rauinous
wolues to axe it from theim as it apperith yn the actes of
th[e] appostles. Is it any merueill though there be nowe so
many beggers, theues, and ydell people? Nay truely.

❡ whate remedy: make lawes ageynst theim. I am yn
doubt whether ye be able: Are they not stronger in your
owne parliament house then your silfe? whate a nombre of
Bisshopes, abbotes, and priours are lordes of your parliament?
are not all the lerned men in your realme in fee with theim
to speake yn your parliament house for theim ageinst your
crowne, dignitie, and comon welth of your realme a fewe of
youre owne lerned counsell onely excepted? whate lawe can
be made ageinst theim that may be aduaylable? who is he
(though he be greued never so sore) for the murdre of his
auncestre rauisshement of his wyfe, of his doughter, robbery,
trespas, maiheme, dette, or eny other offence dare ley it

theyre charge by any wey of accion, and if he do then is he
by and by by theyre wilynesse accused of heresie. ye[a] they
will so handle him or he passe that except he will bere a
fagot for theyre pleasure he shal be excommunicate and then
be all his accions dasshed. So captyue are your lawes vnto
theym that no man that they lyst to excommunicat may be
admitted to sue any accion in any of your courtes. If eny
man yn your sessions dare be so hardy to endyte a prest of eny
suche cryme he hath or the yere [cre he] go out suche a yoke of
heresye leyd in his necke that it maketh him wisshe that he
had not done it. Your grace may se whate a worke there is
in London, howe the bisshoppe rageth for endyting of certayn
curates of extorcion and incontinency the last yere in the
warmoll quest. Had not Richard hunne commenced accyon
of premunire ageinst a prest he had bin yet a lyue and none
heretik at all but an honest man.

 ⸿ Dyd not dyuers of your noble progenitours seynge
theyre crowne and dignite runne ynto ruyne and to be thus
craftely translated ynto the hondes of this myscheuous generacyon make dyuers statutes for the reformacyon therof,
emong whiche the statute of mortmayne was one? to the
intent that after that tyme they shulde haue no more gyuen
vnto theim. But whate avayled it? haue they not gotten
ynto theyre hondes more londes sins then eny duke in
ynglond hath, the statute notwithstonding? Ye[a] haue they
not for all t ıat translated ynto theyre hondes from your grace
half your kyngdome thoroughly? The hole name as reason
is for the auncientie of your kingdome whiche was bifore
theyrs and out of the whiche theyrs is growen onely abiding
with your grace? and of one kyngdome made tweyne: the
spirituall kyngdome (as they call it) for they wyll be named
first, And your temporall kingdome, And whiche of these, ij.
kingdomes suppose ye is like to ouergrowe the other, ye[a] to
put the other clere out of memory? Truely the kingdome of
the bloudsuppers for to theym is giuen daily out of your kingdome. And that that is ones gyuen theim comith neuer from
theim agein. Suche lawes haue they that none of theim may
nether gyue nor sell nothing.

 [⸿] whate lawe can be made so stronge ageinst theim that
they other with money or elles with other policy will not
breake and set at nought? whate kingdome can endure that

euer gyuith thus from him and receyueth nothing agein ?
O howe all the substaunce of your Realme forthwith your
swerde, power, crowne, dignite, and obedience of your
people, rynneth hedlong ynto the insaciabill whyrlepole of
these gredi goulafres to be swalowed and devoured.

℆ Nether haue they eny other coloure to gather these
yerely exaccions ynto theyre hondes but that they sey they
pray for vs to God to delyuer our soules out of the paynes of
purgatori without whose prayer they sey or at lest without
the popes pardon we coude neuer be deliuered thens whiche
if it be true then is it good reason that we gyue theim all
these thinges all were it C times as moche, But there be
many men of greate litterature and iudgement that for the
love they haue vnto the trouth and vnto the comen welth
haue not feared to put theim silf ynto the greatest infamie
that may be, in abiection of all the world, ye[a] in perill of
deth to declare theyre oppinion in this mather whiche is that
there is no purgatory but that it is a thing inuented by
the couitousnesse of the spiritualtie onely to translate all
kingdomes from other princes vnto theim and that there is not
one word spoken of hit is al holy scripture. They sey also
that if there were a purgatory And also if that the pope
with his pardons for money may deliuer one soule thens : he
may deliuer him aswel without money, if he may deliuer
one, he may deliuer a thousand : yf he may deliuer a thousand he may deliuer theim all, and so destroy purgatory.
And then is he a cruell tyraunt without all charite if he kepe
theim there in pryson and in paine till men will giue him
money.

℆ Lyke wyse saie they of all the hole sort of the spiritueltie
that if they will not pray for no man but for theim that gyue
theim money they are tyrauntes and lakke charite, and suffer
those soules to be punisshed and payned vncheritably for
lacke of theyre prayers.   These sort of folkes they call
heretikes, these they burne, these they rage ageinst, put to
open shame and make theim bere fagottes. But whether they
be heretikes or no, well I wote that this purgatory and the
Popes pardons is all the cause of translacion of your kingdome
so fast into their hondes wherfore it is manifest it can not be
of christ, for he gaue more to the temporall kingdome, he
hym silfe paid tribute to Cesar he toke nothing from hym but

taught that the highe powers shulde be alweys obei[e]d ye[a]
he him silf (although he were most fre lorde of all and
innocent) was obedient vnto the highe powers vnto deth. This
is the great scabbe why they will not let the newe testament go
a brode yn your moder tong lest men shulde espie that they
by theyre cloked ypochrisi do translate thus fast your kingdome into theyre hondes, that they are not obedient vnto
your highe power, that they are cruell, vnclene, vnmerciful,
and ypochrites, that thei seke not the honour of Christ but
their owne, that remission of sinnes are not giuen by the
popes pardon, but by Christ, for the sure feith and trust that
we haue in him. Here may your grace well perceyue that
except ye suffer theyre ypocrisie to be disclosed all is like to
runne ynto theire hondes and as long as it is couered so long
shall it seme to euery man to be a greate ympiete not to gyue
theim. For this I am sure your grace thinketh (as the truth
is) I am as good as my father, whye may I not aswell gyue
theim as moche as my father did. And of this mynd I am sure
are all the loordes knightes squir[e]s gentilmen and ye[o]men
in englond, ye[a] and vntill it be disclosed all your peoole [*people*]
will thinke that your statute of mortmayne was neuer made
with no good conscience seing that it taketh awey the liberte
of your people in that they may not as laufully b[u]y theire
soules out of purgatory by gyuing to the spiritualte as their
predecessours did in tymes passed.

℃ wherfore if ye will eschewe the ruyne of your crowne and
dignitie let their ypocrisye be vttered and that shalbe more
spedfull in this mater then all the lawes that may be made
be they never so stronge. For to make a lawe for to punisshe
eny offender except it were more fit to giue other men an
ensample to beware to committe suche like offence, whate shuld
yt auayle. Did not doctour Alyn most presumptuously nowe
yn your tyme ageynst all this allegiaunce all that ever he
coude to pull from you the knowledge of suche plees as [be]long
vnto your hyghe courtes vnto an other court in derogacion
of your crowne and dignite ? Did not also doctor Horsey
and his complices most heynously as all the world knoweth
murdre in pryson that honest marchaunt Richard hunne ? For
that he sued your writ of premunire against a prest that
wrongfully held him in ple[a] in a spirituall court for a mater
wherof the knowlege belonged vnto your hyghe courtes. And

whate punisshement was there done that eny man may take
example of to be ware of lyke offence? truely none but that the
one payd fiue hundreth poundes (as it is said to the b[u]ildinge
of your sterre chamber) and when that payment was ones
passed the capteyns of his kingdome (because he faught so
manfully ageynst your crowne and dignitie) haue heped to
him benefice vpon benefice so that he is rewarded tenne
tymes as moche. The other as it is seid payde sixe hundreth
poundes for him and his complices whiche forbicause that he
had lyke wyse faught so manfully ageynst your crowne and
dignite was ymmediatly (as he had opteyned your most
gracyous pardon) promoted by the capiteynes of his kingdome with benefice vpon benefice to the value of. iiij. tymes
as moche. who can take example of this punisshement to be
ware of suche like offence? who is he of theyre kingdome
that will not rather take courage to committe lyke offence
seying the promocions that fill [fell] to this [these] men for
theyre so offending. So weke and blunt is your swerde to
strike at one of the offenders of this cro[o]ked and peruers
generacyon.

¶ And this is by the reason that the chief instrument of
youre lawe ye[a] the chief of your counsell and he whiche hath
youre swerde in his hond to whome also all the other instrumentes are obedient is alweys a spirituell man whiche hath
euer suche an inordinate loue vnto his owne kingdome that
he will mainteyn that, though all the temporall kingdoms
and comonwelth[s] of the worlde shulde therfore vtterly be
vndone, Here leue we out the gretest mater of all lest that we
declaring suche an horrible carayn of euyll ageinst the
ministres of iniquite shulde seme to declare the one onely
faute or rather the ignoraunce of oure best beloued ministre
of rightousnesse whiche is to be hid till he may be lerned by
these small enormitees that we haue spoken of to knowe it
pleynly him silf. But whate remedy to releue vs your poore
sike lame and sore bedemen? To make many hospitals for
the relief of the poore people? Nay truely. The moo the
worse, for euer the fatte of the hole foundacion hangeth on
the prestes berdes. Dyuers of your noble predecessours
kinges of this realme haue gyuen londes to monasteries to
giue a certein somme of money yerely to the poore people
wherof for the aunciente of the tyme they giue neuer one

peny, They haue lyke wyse giuen to them to haue a certeyn masses said daily for theim wherof they sey neuer one. If the Abbot of westminster shulde sing euery day as many masses for his founders as he is bounde to do by his foundacion. M, monkes were to[o] fewe. wherfore if your grace will bilde a sure hospitall that neuer shall faile to releue vs all your poore bedemen, so take from theim all these thynges. Set these sturdy lobies a brode in the world to get theim wiues of theire owne, to get theire liuing with their laboure in the swete of theire faces according to the commaundement of god. Gene. iij. to gyue other idell people by theire example occasion to go to laboure. Tye these holy idell theues to the cartes to be whipped naked about euery market towne til they will fall to laboure that they by theyre importunate begging take not awey the almesse that the good christen people wolde giue vnto vs sore impotent miserable people your bedemen. Then shall aswell the nombre of oure forsaid monstruous sort as of the baudes, hores, theues, and idell people decreace. Then shall these great yerely exaccions cease. Then shall not youre swerde, power, crowne, dignite, and obedience of your people, be translated from you. Then shall you haue full obedience of your people. Then shall the idell people be set to worke. Then shall matrimony be moche better kept. Then shal the generation of your people be encreased, Then shall your comons encrease in richnesse. Then shall the gospell be preached. Then shall none begge oure almesse from vs. Then shal we haue ynough and more then shall suffice vs, whiche shall be the best hospitall that euer was founded for vs, Then shall we daily pray to god for your most noble estate long to endure.

Domine saluum fac regem.

14

UNWIN BROTHERS, THE GRESHAM PRESS, CHILWORTH AND LONDON.

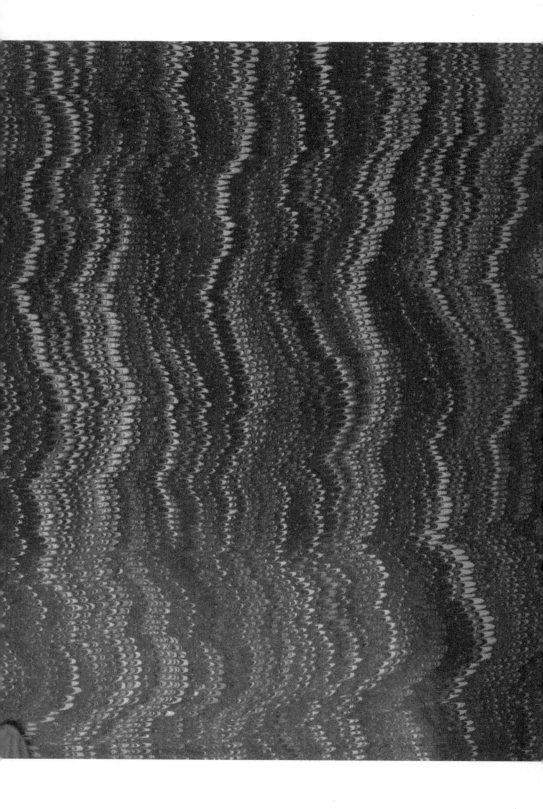